The Central American Cookbook

Authentic Central American Recipes
from Belize, Guatemala, El Salvador,
Honduras, Nicaragua, Costa Rica,
Panama, and Colombia
(3rd Edition)

By
BookSumo Press
All rights reserved

Published by:
http://www.booksumo.com

LEGAL NOTES

All Rights Reserved. No Part Of This Book May Be Reproduced Or Transmitted In Any Form Or By Any Means. Photocopying, Posting Online, And / Or Digital Copying Is Strictly Prohibited Unless Written Permission Is Granted By The Book's Publishing Company. Limited Use Of The Book's Text Is Permitted For Use In Reviews Written For The Public.

Table of Contents

Belize City Rice and Beans 5

Central American Chicken and Cabbage Soup 6

Belizean Belmopan Beach Pudding 7

Chilaquilas: Corn Tortillas Central American Style 8

Guatemalan Pepian: Spicy Sauce for Meats and Rice 9

Full Guatemalan Dinner: Chicken and Potatoes with Sauce 10

Lentils from Santa Ana 11

El Salvador Cabbage Salad 12

Guatemala City Full Rice 13

Maria Rivera's Whole Chicken 14

Spanish Corn Stew 15

Easy Carne Asada 16

Belizean Fried Shrimp 17

Costa Rican Spicy Mayo 18

Light Flour Tortilla Guatemalan Lunch 19

San Pedro Town Pollo Stew 20

Latin Flank Steak 21

Guatemalan Appetizer: Fried Beans and Platanos 22

Arroz y Gandules: Rice and Pigeon Peas 23

Latin Lentils 24

Sweet Beef Ribs 25

Lorna's Chorreagas: Potatoes with Salsa 26

Sancocho: Latin Soup with Salsa 27

Lunch Box Arepas 29

Carne Guisada 101 30

Pollo de Coco: Spicy Coconut Chicken 31

How to Make Plantain 32

Pao de Queijo: Authentic Cheese Rolls 33

Papas Rellenas II: Potato Croquettes 34

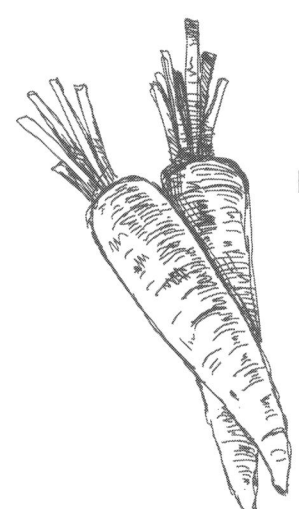

Latin Beef Ribs 35

Central American Cornmeal Cakes 36

Asopao de Pollo: Chicken and Rice Stew 37

Pudim de Leite Condensado: Creamy Flan 38

Habichuelas Guisadas: Latin Bean Stew 39

Arroz con Pollo: Rice and Chicken 40

Tres Leches: Spanish 3 Milk Cake 41

Sofrito Spanish: Spice Mix 42

Tostones: Spanish Plantains Fried 43

Bistec Encebollao Steak and Onions 44

Bacalao Vizcaina: Codfish Soup 45

Classical Spanish Beef Patties 46

Pupusas: Cheese Quesadillas from Salvador 47

Karen's Spicy Chicken 48

Costa Rican 5-Ingredient Potato Salad 49

Jibarito: Sandwich in Fried Plantains Buns 50

Full Latin Dinner: Chicken and Rice 51

San Salvador Butterflied White Fish 52

Arroz con Pollo: Rice and Chicken II 53

Platanos Maduros: Fried Bananas II 54

Carne Con Papas: Beef With Potatoes 55

Honduran Baleadas Avocado and Fried Bean Tacos 56

Honduran Chicken Tacos with Tomato Sauce 57

Bebida de Avena: South American Sweet Oat Drink 58

Easy Picadillo (Ground Beef and Plantains) 59

Isabella's Secret Belize BBQ Sauce 60

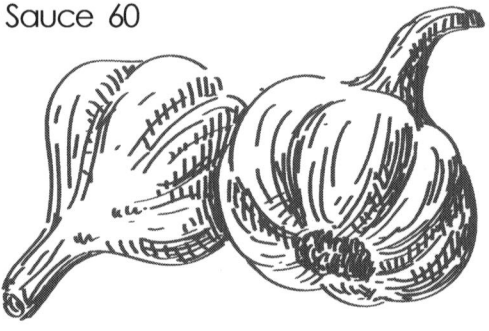

Belize City
Rice and Beans

Prep Time: 15 mins
Total Time: 9 hrs 50 mins

Servings per Recipe: 16
Calories   168 kcal
Fat   2.9 g
Cholesterol   28.5g
Sodium   7.6 g
Carbohydrates   0 mg
Protein   78 mg

Ingredients
Stew Beans:
1 lb dry kidney beans
3 cloves garlic, minced
1/2 onion, chopped
1/2 red bell pepper, chopped
1 tsp vegetable oil
1/2 tsp salt
1/4 tsp ground black pepper
Rice:

1 C. white rice
3/4 C. coconut milk
3/4 C. water

Directions
1. In a large bowl of the water, soak the kidney beans for about 8 hours to overnight.
2. Drain the beans well.
3. In a large pan, add the beans and enough water to cover and bring to a boil.
4. Add the garlic and stir to combine.
5. Reduce the heat to low and simmer for about 1 hour.
6. Stir in the onion, red bell pepper, vegetable oil, salt, black pepper and rice and simmer for about 3 minutes.
7. Stir in the coconut milk, water and kidney beans and bring to a boil on high heat.
8. Reduce the heat to low and simmer, covered for about 30-40 minutes.

CENTRAL AMERICAN Chicken and Cabbage Soup

Prep Time: 15 mins
Total Time: 2 hrs 25 mins

Servings per Recipe: 8
Calories 248 kcal
Fat 8.5 g
Cholesterol 16.3g
Sodium 27.3 g
Carbohydrates 68 mg
Protein 997 mg

Ingredients

- 3 tbsp olive oil
- 2 lb. skinless, boneless chicken breast halves
- seasoned salt to taste
- 6 C. chicken broth
- 1 head green cabbage, shredded
- 1 large onion, chopped
- 1 C. chopped carrots
- 1 green bell pepper, chopped
- 2 stalks celery, chopped
- 1/2 C. chopped cilantro
- 1 (6.5 oz.) can tomato sauce
- 2 limes, juiced
- 4 cloves garlic, minced
- 1 dash hot sauce
- salt and ground black pepper to taste

Directions

1. Season the chicken breast halves with the seasoned salt.
2. In a large Dutch oven, heat the olive oil on medium heat and cook the chicken breast halves for about 5 minutes per side.
3. Stir in the chicken broth, cabbage, onion, carrots, green bell pepper, celery, cilantro, tomato sauce, lime juice, garlic, hot sauce, salt and black pepper and simmer for about 2 hours.
4. Serve hot.

Belize
Belmopan Beach Pudding

Prep Time: 10 mins
Total Time: 1 hrs 10 mins

Servings per Recipe: 12
Calories	409 kcal
Fat	20.1 g
Cholesterol	45g
Sodium	8.4 g
Carbohydrates	67 mg
Protein	386 mg

Ingredients

- 2 eggs
- 1 (12 fluid oz.) can evaporated milk
- 12 fluid oz. coconut milk
- 6 fluid oz. sweetened condensed milk
- 4 fluid oz. apple cider
- 1/2 C. white sugar
- 1/2 C. melted butter
- 1/4 C. raisins
- 2 tsp vanilla extract
- 1 tsp ground nutmeg
- 1 tsp ground cinnamon
- 1 loaf bread, torn in pieces

Directions

1. Set your oven to 250 degrees F before doing anything else and grease a 13x9-inch baking dish.
2. In a large bowl, add the eggs and beat till frothy.
3. Add the evaporated milk, coconut milk, sweetened condensed milk, apple cider, sugar, butter, raisins, vanilla extract, nutmeg and cinnamon and mix till well combined.
4. Fold in the bread pieces.
5. Transfer the mixture into the prepared baking dish evenly.
6. Cook in the oven for about 1 hour.

CHILAQUILAS
Corn Tortillas
(Central American Style)

Prep Time: 25 mins
Total Time: 35 mins

Servings per Recipe: 6
Calories	335 kcal
Fat	19.6 g
Cholesterol	29.3g
Sodium	12.3 g
Carbohydrates	80 mg
Protein	123 mg

Ingredients
1 large tomato, quartered
1 red onion, quartered
1 (12 oz.) package queso fresco, cut into chunks
12 thick corn tortillas
2 eggs, separated
5 tbsp canola oil

Directions
1. In a food processor, add the tomato and red onion and pulse till a paste forms, slowly adding the queso fresco.
2. Fold the corn tortillas in half and fill each with the tomato and red onion paste.
3. In a bowl, add the egg whites and with an electric mixer, beat till foamy.
4. Add the egg yolks, one at a time and beat till well combined.
5. In a large skillet, heat 2-3 tbsp of the oil over medium heat.
6. Coat 1 filled tortilla with the egg mixture evenly and let the excess drip back into the bowl.
7. Cook the tortilla in hot oil for about 2 minutes per side.
8. Repeat with the remaining oil and filled tortillas.

Guatemalan Pepian
(Spicy Sauce for Meats and Rice)

Prep Time: 30 mins
Total Time: 1 hrs 20 mins

Servings per Recipe: 6
Calories   319 kcal
Fat   13.6 g
Cholesterol   44.6 g
Sodium   8.4 g
Carbohydrates   5 mg
Protein   1386 mg

Ingredients
- 6 tomatoes
- 8 fresh tomatillos, husks removed
- 1 onion, peeled
- 2 garlic cloves
- 2 tbsp sesame seeds
- 2 tbsp hulled pumpkin seeds
- 1 thick slice of French baguette
- 4 sprigs fresh cilantro
- 1 tsp salt
- 2 black peppercorns
- 3 C. chicken broth
- 1/4 C. olive oil
- 1 chayote, cut into 8 pieces
- 4 potatoes, thickly sliced
- 1 C. fresh corn kernels
- 3 C. chicken broth

Directions
1. Heat a large skillet on medium-high heat and cook the tomatoes, tomatillos, onion and garlic for about 20 minutes.
2. With a slotted spoon, transfer the vegetables into a bowl.
3. In the same skillet, add the sesame and pumpkin seeds and stir fry for about 2-3 minutes.
4. Remove from the heat.
5. In a toaster, toast the baguette slice.
6. In a blender, add the baguette slice, tomatoes, onion, garlic, sesame seeds, cilantro, salt and black peppercorns
7. Add 3 C. of the chicken broth and pulse till smooth.
8. Through a sieve, strain the blended sauce completely.
9. In a large pan, mix together the sauce and olive oil on medium-high heat and bring to a boil.
10. Cook for about 3 minutes.
11. Stir in the chayote, potatoes, corn and 3 C. of the chicken broth and bring to a boil.
12. Reduce the heat to low and simmer for about 20 minutes.

FULL GUATEMALAN
Dinner
(Chicken and Potatoes with Sauce)

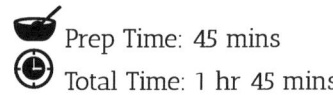

Prep Time: 45 mins
Total Time: 1 hr 45 mins

Servings per Recipe: 6
Calories	407 kcal
Fat	18.1 g
Cholesterol	46.1g
Sodium	18.5 g
Carbohydrates	43 mg
Protein	467 mg

Ingredients
1 lb. chicken thighs
3 zucchini, thickly sliced
4 potatoes, cut into chunks
2 carrots, sliced
5 C. chicken broth
1 tsp salt
For Pulique Sauce:
1/4 C. masa harina flour
2 tbsp water
6 tomatoes, cored and cut into chunks
6 large fresh tomatillos, husks removed
2 cloves garlic, cut in half
1 onion, cut into chunks
3 dried guajillo Chile peppers, stems and seeds removed
1 (1 inch) piece cinnamon stick
6 whole cumin seeds
2 whole cloves
2 black peppercorns
3 tbsp dried epazote (Mexican tea leaves), or any tea leaves
2 tsp achiote seed
1/4 C. olive oil
salt to taste

Directions
1. In a large pan, add the chicken thighs, zucchini, potatoes, carrots, chicken broth and 1 tsp of the salt and bring to a boil.
2. Reduce the heat and simmer for about 20 minutes.
3. With a slotted spoon, transfer the chicken and vegetables into a bowl, reserving the broth in the pan.
4. In a small bowl, dissolve the masa harina in water and keep aside for about 10 minutes.
5. Make a 2-inch ball from the masa dough.
6. Add the dough ball, tomatoes, tomatillos, garlic, onion, guajillo peppers, cinnamon stick, cumin seeds, cloves, peppercorns, and epazote and achiote seed in the broth and bring to a boil.
7. Reduce the heat and simmer for about 20 minutes.
8. Discard the cinnamon stick.
9. Through a strainer, strain the mixture, reserving 1/2 C. of the broth.
10. In a blender, add the tomato mixture and dough ball and pulse till smooth.
11. Through a strainer, strain the sauce and keep aside.
12. In a large pan, heat the olive oil on medium heat.
13. Slowly, add the sauce and fry for about 3 minutes.
14. Stir in the cooked chicken, vegetables, reserved chicken broth and salt.
15. Reduce the heat to low and simmer for about 10 minutes.

Lentils from Santa Ana

Prep Time: 10 mins
Total Time: 55 mins

Servings per Recipe: 3
Calories	201 kcal
Fat	5.3 g
Cholesterol	31.1g
Sodium	9.3 g
Carbohydrates	0 mg
Protein	789 mg

Ingredients

- 1/2 C. lentils
- 1 1/2 C. water
- 1 small tomato, chopped
- 1 small onion, chopped
- 2 tsp ground cumin
- 1 tsp salt
- 1 tbsp vegetable oil
- 2 small yellow potatoes, cubed

Directions

1. In a pan, mix together the lentils, water, tomato, onion, cumin, salt and vegetable oil on medium heat and bring to a boil.
2. Cook for about 30 minutes.
3. Add the potatoes and cook for about 15 minutes.

EL SALVADOR
Cabbage Salad

🥣 Prep Time: 20 mins
🕒 Total Time: 45 mins

Servings per Recipe: 4
Calories   50 kcal
Fat   0.3 g
Cholesterol   < 11.3g
Sodium   2.3 g
Carbohydrates   0 mg
Protein   47 mg

Ingredients
1/2 head green cabbage, cored and shredded
1 carrot, grated
1 quart boiling water
3 green onions, minced
1 C. distilled white vinegar
1/2 C. water
2 tsp dried oregano

Directions
1. In a large bowl, add the cabbage, carrot and boiling water and steep for about 5 minutes.
2. Drain well.
3. Return the cabbage, carrots into the bowl with the green onion, vinegar, 1/2 C. of the water and oregano and toss to coat well.
4. Refrigerate to chill for about 20 minutes before serving.

Guatemala City
Full Rice

🥣 Prep Time: 10 mins
🕐 Total Time: 30 mins

Servings per Recipe: 2	
Calories	440 kcal
Fat	11.1 g
Cholesterol	75.8g
Sodium	7.1 g
Carbohydrates	< 1 mg
Protein	< 392 mg

Ingredients

- 1 1/2 tbsp vegetable oil
- 1 C. long-grain rice
- 1 tbsp minced onion
- 1 tbsp minced tomato
- 2 C. water
- 2 tbsp chopped carrot
- 1 tbsp chopped celery
- 2 tsp chicken bouillon granules

Directions

1. In a large skillet, heat the oil on medium-high heat and cook the rice, onion and tomato for about 3-4 minutes.
2. Stir in the water, carrot, celery and chicken bouillon and simmer for about 8 minutes.
3. Simmer, covered for about 5-8 minutes.

MARIA RIVERA'S
Whole Chicken

Prep Time: 15 mins
Total Time: 1 hr 40 mins

Servings per Recipe: 6
Calories   429 kcal
Fat   27.6 g
Cholesterol   13.8g
Sodium   32 g
Carbohydrates   97 mg
Protein   576 mg

Ingredients
- 1 (3 lb.) whole chicken, cut into pieces
- 1 lemon, juiced
- 1/4 C. olive oil
- 1 tsp salt
- 1/2 tsp ground black pepper
- 3/4 tsp paprika
- 1 (2.25 oz.) can sliced black olives, drained
- 1 large onion, chopped
- 1 medium green bell pepper, sliced
- 1 medium red bell pepper, sliced
- 1 1/2 C. orange juice

Directions
1. In a bowl, add the chicken pieces and drizzle with the lemon juice.
2. Refrigerate, covered for at least 30 minutes.
3. Set your oven to 350 degrees F.
4. In a small bowl, mix together the salt, pepper and paprika.
5. Sprinkle the spice mixture over the chicken pieces evenly.
6. In a skillet, heat the olive oil on medium-high heat and sear the chicken pieces till browned from both sides.
7. Transfer the chicken pieces into a baking dish and top with the olives, onion, green bell pepper and red bell pepper evenly.
8. Place the orange juice on top evenly.
9. With a piece of the foil, cover the baking dish and cook in the oven for about 45 minutes.

Spanish Corn Stew

🥣 Prep Time: 30 mins
🕐 Total Time: 2 hrs

Servings per Recipe: 6
Calories   693 kcal
Fat   28.8 g
Cholesterol   71.3g
Sodium   41.1 g
Carbohydrates   104 mg
Protein   714 mg

Ingredients

1 (3 lb.) whole chicken, cut into pieces
8 potatoes, peeled and cubed
1 onion, chopped
1 tsp salt
1 tsp ground black pepper
1/2 tsp garlic powder
1 (15.25 oz.) can whole kernel corn, drained
2 avocados, peeled, pitted, and diced
1/4 C. chopped fresh cilantro
sour cream, for topping

Directions

1. In a large pan, add the chicken pieces and enough water to cover on medium heat and bring to a boil.
2. Simmer for about 45 minutes.
3. Transfer the chicken into a bowl, reserving the water in the pan.
4. Keep the chicken aside to cool slightly.
5. Remove the meat from bones and shred into strands.
6. Return the pan of water to medium heat.
7. Add the potatoes, onion, salt, pepper and garlic powder and cook for about 30 minutes.
8. With a potato masher, mash the potatoes into the broth till a thick mixture is formed.
9. Stir in the shredded chicken and corn and cook till heated completely.
10. Stir in the avocado and cilantro and serve with a topping of the sour cream.

EASY
Carne Asada

🥣 Prep Time: 25 mins
🕐 Total Time: 2 hr 35 mins

Servings per Recipe: 4
Calories   236 kcal
Fat   15.6 g
Cholesterol   9.2g
Sodium   15.4 g
Carbohydrates   36 mg
Protein   770 mg

Ingredients
2 tbsp corn oil
1 lb. flank steak
1 large Spanish onion, thinly sliced
4 large cloves garlic, chopped
5 Roma tomatoes, chopped
1/2 tsp salt
2 tsp black pepper
1 1/2 tsp ground cumin
2 1/2 C. water
2 cubes beef bouillon, crumbled

Directions
1. In a skillet, heat the corn oil on medium heat and cook the steak till browned from both sides.
2. Transfer the steak into a plate.
3. In the same skillet, add the onion, garlic, tomatoes, salt, pepper and cumin and sauté till the onion becomes tender.
4. Stir in the crumbled bouillon, steak and water and bring to a boil.
5. Reduce the heat to low and simmer, covered for about 2 hours.
6. With a slotted spoon, transfer the steak onto a cutting board.
7. With 2 forks, shred the steak.
8. Transfer the shredded meat onto a serving plate and top with the onion mixture.
9. Serve immediately.

Belizean Fried Shrimp

🥣 Prep Time: 20 mins
🕐 Total Time: 35 mins

Servings per Recipe: 4
Calories   801.7
Fat   66.4 g
Cholesterol   194 mg
Sodium   737.6 mg
Carbohydrates   31.5 g
Protein   21.1 g

Ingredients

- 1 lb. large shrimp, peeled & cleaned
- 1 egg
- 1/2 C. milk
- 3/4 C. flour
- 1/4 tsp oregano, dried and crumbled
- salt & pepper
- 1 C. shredded coconut
- 1 C. vegetable oil

Directions

1. Cut each shrimp along vein and lay out flat.
2. In a bowl, add the egg, milk, flour and all the seasoning and beat till smooth.
3. Dip each shrimp in egg mixture and then coat with the shredded coconut.
4. Keep aside for about 30 minutes.
5. In a skillet, heat the vegetable oil and deep fry the shrimp till browned.
6. Transfer the bacon onto a paper towel lined plate to drain.
7. Serve hot.

COSTA RICAN
Spicy Mayo

Prep Time: 15 mins
Total Time: 25 mins

Servings per Recipe: 1 bottle
Calories   2045.2
Fat   224 g
Cholesterol   211.5 mg
Sodium   2396.2 mg
Carbohydrates   9.9 g
Protein   7.3 g

Ingredients
1 egg
1/4 tsp cayenne pepper
1 tsp dry mustard
1 tsp salt
1 tsp white sugar
3 tbsp fresh squeezed lemon juice
1 C. vegetable oil

Directions
1. In a blender, add the egg, pepper, salt, mustard, white sugar and half of the oil and pulse on high till smooth.
2. While the motor is running, slowly add the lemon juice and remainder oil and pulse till smooth.

Light Flour Tortilla Guatemalan Lunch

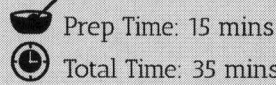

Prep Time: 15 mins
Total Time: 35 mins

Servings per Recipe: 10	
Calories	157.2
Fat	7.8 g
Cholesterol	1 mg
Sodium	355.6 mg
Carbohydrates	17.5 g
Protein	4.2 g

Ingredients
- 1 C. farmer cheese
- 1 small red bell pepper, finely chopped
- 1 small onion, finely chopped
- 1/2 tsp pepper
- 1/2 tsp salt
- 1/4 tsp garlic powder
- 10 flour tortillas
- 1/4 C. olive oil
- salsa

Directions
1. In a bowl, mix together the cheese, pepper, onion, black pepper, salt and garlic powder.
2. Place about 1 heaping tbsp of the cheese mixture over the lower half of each tortilla.
3. Fold the tortilla over the filling to make a half-moon shape and then, press lightly.
4. In a skillet, heat the oil on medium high heat and fry the tortillas till crisp and golden from both sides.
5. Serve warm with salsa.

SAN PEDRO TOWN
Pollo Stew

Prep Time: 15 mins
Total Time: 1 hr 25 mins

Servings per Recipe: 4
Calories   809.3
Fat   57.1g
Cholesterol   243.8mg
Sodium   1695.6mg
Carbohydrates   11.1g
Protein   60.0g

Ingredients
- 1 whole chicken, cut up
- 2 tbsp white vinegar
- 2 tbsp achiote paste
- 1 onion
- 1 green bell pepper
- 5 garlic cloves
- 3 tbsp soy sauce
- 3 tbsp Worcestershire sauce
- 2 tbsp cumin
- 1 tsp thyme
- 1 tsp oregano
- 1 tsp salt
- 1/2 tsp fresh ground black pepper
- 1 - 2 tbsp coconut oil
- 1 - 2 tsp sugar
- water, to cover
- 1 bay leaf

Directions
1. In a small bowl, mix together the achiote paste and vinegar.
2. Rub the achiote paste mixture over the chicken pieces evenly.
3. In a large bowl, add the chicken pieces, Worcestershire sauce, cumin, thyme, oregano and black pepper and mix well.
4. Chop the onion, pepper and garlic and keep aside.
5. In a large pan, melt the coconut oil.
6. Add the sugar and swirl to spread evenly.
7. Remove the chicken from the bowl, reserving the marinade.
8. In the pan, add the chicken pieces and cook till browned from both sides.
9. Add the onions, peppers and garlic and sauté till translucent.
10. Add the reserved marinade and enough water to almost cover the chicken and simmer for about 40-60 minutes.

Latin Flank Steak

Prep Time: 10 mins
Total Time: 3 hrs 10 mins

Servings per Recipe: 6
Calories   331.9
Fat   19.4g
Cholesterol   61.9mg
Sodium   279.4mg
Carbohydrates   5.2g
Protein   32.8g

Ingredients

- 2 lb. flank steaks, trimmed of fat
- 4 small tomatoes, finely chopped
- 1 C. onion, chopped
- 1 tsp garlic, minced
- 1/2 tsp salt
- 3 tbsp olive oil

Directions

1. In a large bowl, mix together 2 tomatoes, 1/4 C. of the onions, 1/2 tsp of the garlic and 1/4 tsp of the salt.
2. Add the flank steak and coat with the mixture generously.
3. Refrigerate for overnight.
4. In a Dutch oven, place the marinated flank steak and enough water to cover and cook, covered for about 2 1/2 hours.
5. Remove the steak from the pan and keep aside to cool.
6. With 2 forks, shred thee meat.
7. In a large skillet, heat the olive oil on medium heat and sauté the remaining onions, tomato, garlic and salt till tender.
8. Add the shredded meat and stir fry for about 10 minutes.

GUATEMALAN
Appetizer
(Fried Beans and Platanos)

Prep Time: 30 mins
Total Time: 1 hr 30 mins

Servings per Recipe: 12
Calories 788.1
Fat 73.4 g
Cholesterol 0 mg
Sodium 357.7 mg
Carbohydrates 35 g
Protein 3.1 g

Ingredients
6 plantains, peeled and broken into chunks
1 (16 oz.) can refried black beans
1 tbsp white sugar
1 tsp salt
1 quart oil (for frying)

Directions
1. In a large pan, add the plantains and enough water to cover and bring to a boil.
2. Reduce the heat and simmer for about 15 minutes.
3. Drain the plantains and mash them.
4. In a small pan, add the refried beans on low heat, sugar and salt and stir till well combined.
5. Remove from the heat.
6. For the rellenitos, make a palm-sized ball from the mashed plantains and flatten each ball.
7. Place about 1 tsp of the bean mixture in the center of each ball and then mold the sides of the plantain around the beans, making an egg-shaped ball.
8. In a large skillet, heat the oil to 375 degrees F and fry the rellenitos in batches till browned completely.
9. Transfer the rellenitos onto a paper towel lined plate to drain.
10. Serve with the sour cream.

Arroz y Gandules
Rice and Pigeon Peas

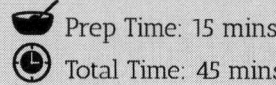 Prep Time: 15 mins
Total Time: 45 mins

Servings per Recipe: 6
Calories   652.1
Fat   6.6g
Cholesterol   0.2mg
Sodium   574.4mg
Carbohydrates   124.9g
Protein   22.6g

Ingredients

- 3 C. rice
- 6 C. water
- 1 (15 oz.) cans green pigeon peas, undrained
- 1 small onion, finely chopped
- 1 medium green bell pepper, finely chopped
- 1 garlic clove, minced
- 1/4 C. coarsely chopped pimento stuffed olive
- 2 tbsp capers
- 1/2 C. finely chopped cilantro (fresh)
- 1 C. chorizo sausage, coarsely chopped
- 2 tbsp vegetable oil
- 3 chicken bouillon cubes
- 1 tsp ground cumin
- 1/4 tsp paprika
- 1/4 tsp salt
- 5 sprigs cilantro

Directions

1. In large, heavy pan, heat the oil on medium heat and sauté the onion and bell pepper for about 2 minutes.
2. Add the gandules, chopped cilantro, garlic, capers, olives and chorizo and sauté for about 2-3 minutes.
3. Add the water, bouillon cubes, cumin, salt and paprika and increase the heat to medium-high.
4. Bring to a boil, stirring continuously.
5. Add the rice and boil for about 3 minutes.
6. Arrange the cilantro the sprigs across the top of the rice.
7. Reduce the heat to low and simmer, covered for about 25 minutes.
8. Remove from the heat and discard the cilantro sprigs.
9. With a fork, fluff the rice and serve.

LATIN Lentils

Prep Time: 15 mins
Total Time: 55 mins

Servings per Recipe: 4
Calories   266 kcal
Fat   4.3 g
Carbohydrates   46.3g
Protein   13.4 g
Cholesterol   0 mg
Sodium   225 mg

Ingredients

1 C. dry lentils
1 quart water
1 cube vegetable bouillon
3 medium tomatoes, peeled and diced
1 large onion, diced
1 carrot, sliced
1 medium apple - peeled, cored and diced
1/2 C. frozen peas
1 large clove garlic
1 tbsp olive oil

1/4 C. barbeque sauce
1/2 tsp paprika
salt and pepper to taste

Directions

1. Combine your water, lentils, and veggie bouillon.
2. Get everything boiling, set the heat to low, and let the mix cook for 22 mins.
3. Add in: paprika, tomatoes, bbq sauce, onions, olive oil, carrots, garlic, peas, and apples.
4. Let the mix continue to cook for 22 more mins then add some pepper and salt.
5. Enjoy.

Sweet Beef Ribs

Prep Time: 2 hrs
Total Time: 50 hrs

Servings per Recipe: 4
Calories 224.5
Fat 0.5g
Cholesterol 0.0mg
Sodium 1249.4mg
Carbohydrates 56.8g
Protein 2.2g

Ingredients

- 1 (14 oz.) bottles ketchup
- 1/2 C. maple syrup
- 3 tbsp balsamic vinegar
- 2 tbsp Worcestershire sauce
- 1 tbsp Dijon mustard
- 1 tbsp fresh minced garlic
- 3 finely chopped green onions
- 1/2 tsp cinnamon
- 1/2 tsp allspice
- 1/4 tsp fresh ground black pepper
- 1 dash hot pepper sauce
- 4 lb. meaty beef ribs

Directions

1. In a large bowl, mix together all the ingredients except the beef ribs.
2. Add the ribs and coat with the sauce generously.
3. Refrigerate, covered for at least 2 hours or as long as 48 hours, flipping occasionally.
4. Set your oven to 325 degrees F.
5. Remove the ribs from the bowl, reserving the sauce.
6. Arrange the ribs in a large roasting pan, bone-side down.
7. Coat the ribs with the sauce and cook in the oven for about 30 minutes.
8. Remove from the oven and turn the ribs over.
9. Coat the ribs with the sauce and cook in the oven for about 30 minutes.
10. Remove from the oven and turn the ribs over.
11. Coat the ribs with the remaining sauce and cook in the oven for about 35-40 minutes, basting occasionally.

LORNA'S CHORREAGAS
Potatoes with Salsa

Prep Time: 10 mins
Total Time: 30 mins

Servings per Recipe: 5
Calories   142.2
Fat   3.9g
Cholesterol   0.1mg
Sodium   252.4mg
Carbohydrates   24.7g
Protein   3.4g

Ingredients

- 1 lb potato, peeled and cut in half lengthwise
- 1 chicken bouillon cube
- salt and freshly ground black pepper
- 1 tbsp olive oil
- 1/2 C. sweet onions, chopped fine
- 2 tomatoes, chopped fine
- 1/4 C. fresh parsley, chopped
- 1 tsp ground cumin
- sazon goya con culantro y achiote
- 1/4 C. queso fresco
- sliced green onion, for garnish

Directions

1. In a pan of the water, cook the potatoes with the chicken bouillon and a little salt till tender.
2. Meanwhile in a skillet, heat the oil on medium heat and cook the onion, tomatoes and parsley till the onion becomes soft.
3. Stir in the cumin, sazon, salt and pepper and remove from the heat.
4. Transfer the cooked potatoes into a serving bowl and top with the tomato mixture evenly and crumbled cheese.
5. Serve with a garnishing of the green onions.

Sancocho
Spanish Soup with Salsa

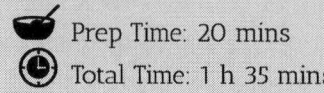

Prep Time: 20 mins
Total Time: 1 h 35 mins

Servings per Recipe: 6
Calories   689.6
Fat   17.9g
Cholesterol   125.4mg
Sodium   1910.0mg
Carbohydrates   88.3g
Protein   49.7g

Ingredients

SALSA (Aji):

1 C. fresh cilantro leaves, finely chopped
8 scallions, finely chopped
1/2 small scotch bonnet pepper, seeded and finely chopped
1 tbsp finely chopped white onion
2 tsp fresh lime juice
3/4 C. water
1 small plum tomato, cored and finely chopped
salt

SOUP:

3 tbsp olive oil
2 large yellow onions, finely chopped
3 garlic cloves, finely minced
2 large tomatoes, cored, peeled, seeded and chopped
3 bay leaves
1 tbsp finely chopped fresh thyme leave
2 lb. skinless chicken thighs, excess fat removed
2 lb. flanken beef ribs
2 green plantains, peeled and cut into 2-inch long pieces
2 ripe plantains, peeled and cut into 2 inch long pieces
1 bunch fresh cilantro, stems tied together with kitchen twine
14 C. chicken broth, homemade
1 1/2 lb. small potatoes, peeled
3 C. diced pumpkin
10 pieces frozen yucca root
4 ears corn, husked and quartered
white rice, for serving
1 medium Hass avocado, halved, seeded, peeled and sliced for serving
6 tortillas, for serving

Directions

1. For the aji in a small glass bowl, add all the ingredients and mix well.
2. Cover and keep aside in the room temperature for several hours.
3. Then, refrigerate before serving.
4. In a large pan, heat the oil on medium heat and sauté the onions and garlic for about 5 minutes.
5. Add the tomatoes, bay leaves and thyme and cook for about 5 minutes.
6. Add the chicken and beef ribs and cook for about 15 minutes, stirring occasionally and skimming the foam from the top surface.
7. Stir in the green plantains, cilantro and chicken stock and bring to a boil.
8. Reduce the the heat to medium-low and simmer, covered for about 30 minutes.
9. With a slotted spoon, transfer the chicken into a bowl and keep aside.
10. Stir in the potatoes, pumpkin, ripe plantains, yucca and corn and simmer, uncovered for about 20 minutes.
11. Remove the cilantro and the bay leaves.
12. Return the chicken to the pan and cook till heated completely.
13. In serving plates, divide the chicken, beef, plantains and vegetables.
14. Transfer the broth in small serving bowls.
15. Serve alongside the aji sauce, rice, corn, avocados and tortillas.

Lunch Box Arepas

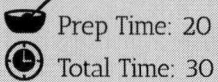

Prep Time: 20 mins
Total Time: 30 mins

Servings per Recipe: 6
Calories   409.4
Fat   22.3g
Cholesterol   76.5mg
Sodium   1322.2mg
Carbohydrates   32.4g
Protein   21.0g

Ingredients

- 2 C. masa harina
- 1 C. grated white cheese
- 1 tsp baking soda
- 1 tsp salt 2 1/2 C. warm water
- 4 -6 tbsp butter, divided

Sandwich:

- 1/2 lb sliced ham
- 1/2 lb mozzarella cheese, cut into 6 slices
- 1 large tomatoes, cut into 6 slices
- 1/4 tsp salt
- 1/4 tsp pepper
- 4 -6 tsp butter, divided
- 1/2 C. salsa

Directions

1. For the Arepas in a large bowl, mix together the masa, cheese, baking soda and salt.
2. Slowly, add the warm water and stir well.
3. With your hands, knead till a smooth dough is formed.
4. Make 6 equal sized balls from the mixture and flatten into 4-inch circles.
5. In a cast iron skillet, melt half of the butter on medium heat and cook the Arepas
6. in batches for about 3 minutes.
7. Add the remaining butter and carefully, flip the Arepas.
8. Cook for about 2-3 minutes.
9. Transfer onto plate and keep aside to cool slightly.
10. Slice the arepas in half horizontally.
11. Palace the ham, cheese and tomato over the cut side of arepas and sprinkle with the salt and pepper.
12. Cover with the remaining Arepas halves.
13. In a skillet, melt half of the butter and cook the Arepas in batches for about 3 minutes.
14. Add the remaining butter and carefully, flip the Arepas.
15. Cook for about 2-3 minutes.
16. Serve alongside the salsa.

CARNE GUISADA 101

Prep Time: 15 mins
Total Time: 2 hrs 15 mins

Servings per Recipe: 5
Calories 194.6
Fat 8.3g
Cholesterol 14.9mg
Sodium 456.8mg
Carbohydrates 22.7g
Protein 7.1g

Ingredients

2 tsp olive oil
1 C. scallion, chopped
3 garlic cloves, minced
2 small tomatoes, chopped
2 tbsp cilantro, minced
1 1/2 lb. choice round beef stew, cut into small chunks
1/3 C. broth, optional

1/3 C. water
1/2 tsp cumin
1/4 tsp adobo seasoning
1/2 tsp achiote
1 bay leaf
salt
10 oz. baby red potatoes, halved

Directions

1. In a large Dutch oven, heat the oil on medium heat and sauté the scallions and garlic for about 2-3 minutes.
2. Add the tomatoes, cilantro and a pinch of salt and cook for about 2 minutes, stirring continuously.
3. Add the beef, broth, water, cumin, adobo, achiote, bay leaf and salt and stir to combine.
4. Reduce the heat to low and simmer, covered for about 1 1/2 hours.
5. Stir in the potatoes and simmer for about 20 minutes.

Pollo de Coco
Spicy Coconut Chicken

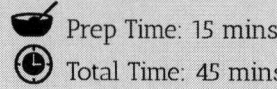
Prep Time: 15 mins
Total Time: 45 mins

Servings per Recipe: 4
Calories	345 kcal
Fat	19.9 g
Carbohydrates	11.5g
Protein	29.3 g
Cholesterol	72 mg
Sodium	234 mg

Ingredients

- 1 tsp ground cumin
- 1 tsp ground cayenne pepper
- 1 tsp ground turmeric
- 1 tsp ground coriander
- 4 skinless, boneless chicken breast halves
- salt and pepper to taste
- 2 tbsp olive oil
- 1 onion, chopped
- 1 tbsp minced fresh ginger
- 2 jalapeno peppers, seeded and chopped
- 2 cloves garlic, minced
- 3 tomatoes, seeded and chopped
- 1 (14 oz.) can light coconut milk
- 1 bunch chopped fresh parsley

Directions

1. In a bowl, mix together the cumin, cayenne pepper, turmeric, coriander, salt and pepper.
2. Add the chicken and rub with the spice mixture evenly.
3. In a skillet, heat 1 tbsp of the oil on medium heat and cook the chicken for about 10-15 minutes per side.
4. Remove from the heat and keep aside.
5. In the same skillet, heat the remaining oil and Cook and stir the onion, ginger, jalapeño peppers and garlic for about 5 minutes.
6. Stir in the tomatoes and cook for about 5-8 minutes.
7. Stir in the coconut milk and pour over the chicken.
8. Serve with a garnishing of the parsley.

HOW TO MAKE
Plantains

Prep Time: 5 mins
Total Time: 20 mins

Servings per Recipe: 4
Calories 218.3
Fat 0.6g
Cholesterol 0.0mg
Sodium 7.1mg
Carbohydrates 57.0g
Protein 2.3g

Ingredients
4 plantains
cooking spray

Directions
1. Set your oven to 350 degrees F before doing anything else and grease a baking sheet with the cooking spray.
2. Cut the ends off of each plantains and peel.
3. Cut each plantain on the diagonal into 1/2-inch slices.
4. Arrange the plantain slices onto the prepared baking sheet in a single layer.
5. With the cooking spray, coat the tops f the plantain slices.
6. Cook in the oven for about 10-15 minutes, flipping occasionally.

Pao de Queijo Authentic Cheese Rolls

Prep Time: 20 mins
Total Time: 45 mins

Servings per Recipe: 14
Calories   199 kcal
Fat   12 g
Carbohydrates   17.2g
Protein   5.8 g
Cholesterol   36 mg
Sodium   386 mg

Ingredients

- 2 C. tapioca starch
- 1 tsp salt
- 1/2 C. vegetable oil
- 1/3 C. water
- 1/3 C. milk
- 2 eggs
- 6 oz. shredded Parmesan cheese

Directions

1. Set your oven to 375 degrees F before doing anything else and lightly, grease a baking sheet.
2. In a large bowl, add the tapioca starch and salt.
3. In a pan, add the vegetable oil, water and milk and bring to a boil on medium heat till a white foam appears.
4. Place the milk mixture over the tapioca starch and stir till well combined and keep aside for about 15 minutes.
5. Add the eggs and Parmesan cheese and mix till well combined.
6. Make about 1 1/2-inch balls from the dough and arrange on the prepared baking sheet.
7. Cook in the oven for about 15-20 minutes.

PAPAS RELLENAS II
Potato Croquettes

 Prep Time: 30 mins
Total Time: 1 hrs

Servings per Recipe: 4
Calories 332.9
Fat 19.5g
Cholesterol 61.8mg
Sodium 56.1mg
Carbohydrates 25.3g
Protein 14.4g

Ingredients
- 2 1/4 lb. potatoes
- salt & freshly ground black pepper
- 1 fresh egg
- 3 hard-boiled eggs, chopped
- 6 tbsp oil
- 1 lb ground beef
- 1 C. onion, chopped
- 2 garlic cloves, minced
- 1 tbsp paprika
- 6 stuffed green olives, cut in 4
- 1/2 C. tomatoes, peeled, seeded and diced
- 1 tsp fresh parsley, minced
- 1 tsp cilantro, minced
- 1/4 C. golden raisin

Directions
In a large pan of salted water, boil the potatoes for about 20 minutes.

Drain the potatoes and keep aside to cool slightly.

Remove the peel of the potatoes and mash the.

Keep the potatoes aside to come to near room temperature.

Add 1 egg and knead till smooth and soft.

In a large skillet, heat 2-3 tbsp of the oil on medium heat and cook the onions and garlic for about 5-7 minutes.

Add ground beef and tomatoes and cook for about 5 minutes, breaking up with a wooden spoon.

Stir in the parsley, cilantro, olives, hard boiled eggs, raisins, salt, pepper and paprika and remove from the heat.

Take about 3/4 C. of the potato mixture and flatten in your hand.

Place about 2 tbsp of the meat filling in the center.

Carefully fold over the filling and pinch closed to form an oval shape.

Coat each oval with the flour and keep aside.

Repeat with the remaining ingredients.

Refrigerate for about 20 minutes.

In a deep fryer, heat the remaining oil and fry the rellenas till golden brown from all the sides.

Transfer the rellenas onto a paper towel lined plate to drain

Latin Beef Ribs

Prep Time: 10 mins
Total Time: 6 hrs 20 mins

Servings per Recipe: 10
Calories	698 kcal
Fat	56.5 g
Carbohydrates	0 g
Protein	44.1 g
Cholesterol	163 mg
Sodium	3647 mg

Ingredients

- 1 (3 lb.) rack of whole beef ribs (not short ribs)
- 2 tbsp sea salt, or more if needed
- 3/4 C. water

Directions

1. Set your oven to 275 degrees F before doing anything else.
2. Place the rack of beef ribs on a work surface with the shiny white membrane facing up.
3. Slip the blade of a sharp knife under the membrane at one end, and slice the membrane off the meat in a single piece.
4. Discard the chewy membrane and rub the ribs with the salt evenly.
5. Arrange the ribs onto a cooking rack in a roasting pan.
6. Cook in the oven for about 1 1/2 hours.
7. Lightly baste the beef with the water.
8. Cook for 4 1/2 hours more, Basting after every 45 minutes.
9. Remove from the oven and keep aside to cool for about 10-15 minutes before slicing.

CENTRAL AMERICAN
Cornmeal Cakes

🥣 Prep Time: 10 mins
🕒 Total Time: 40 mins

Servings per Recipe: 6
Calories 508 kcal
Fat 18.3 g
Carbohydrates 79.2g
Protein 8.1 g
Cholesterol 72 mg
Sodium 106 mg

Ingredients

- 2 C. cornmeal
- 1 1/2 C. white sugar
- 1 C. milk
- 1 C. coconut milk
- 1 C. all-purpose flour
- 3 eggs
- 1/3 C. vegetable oil
- 1 tsp baking powder

Directions

1. Set your oven to 340 degrees F before doing anything else and grease and flour a 10-inch cake pan.
2. In a blender, add the cornmeal, sugar, milk, coconut milk, flour, eggs and vegetable oil and pulse till smooth.
3. Add the baking powder and pulse till well combined.
4. Transfer the cornmeal mixture into the prepared cake pan.
5. Cook in the oven for about 30-40 minutes or till a toothpick inserted into the center comes out clean.

Asopao de Pollo
Chicken and Rice Stew

Prep Time: 25 mins
Total Time: 1 hr

Servings per Recipe: 6
Calories	550 kcal
Fat	17.7 g
Carbohydrates	55.2g
Protein	38.1 g
Cholesterol	131 mg
Sodium	2149 mg

Ingredients

- 2 lbs boneless, skinless chicken thighs
- ½ tsp ground black pepper
- 1 serving light adobo seasoning
- 3 tbsps olive oil
- 1 green bell pepper, diced
- 1 red bell pepper, diced
- 1 medium onion, diced
- 4 cloves garlic, minced
- 2 tbsps tomato paste
- 1 ½ C. medium grain rice
- 2 cans diced tomatoes
- 6 C. chicken broth
- 1 bay leaf
- ¼ tsp red pepper flakes, or to taste
- 1 C. frozen petite peas, thawed
- 1 C. sliced pimento-stuffed green olives
- ¼ C. diced fresh cilantro

Directions

1. Coat your pieces of chicken with adobo and pepper.
2. Now begin to stir fry your tomato paste, green pepper, garlic, red pepper, and onions in hot oil for 5 mins. Now place everything to the side.
3. Sear your chicken for 6 mins per side then add back in the onion mix.
4. Also add in: pepper flakes, rice, bay leaf, broth, and diced tomatoes.
5. Get everything boiling then set the heat to a low level and cook the mix for 22 mins until the chicken is fully done and the rice is soft.
6. Now add the olives and peas.
7. Cook everything for 7 more mins then remove the bay leaf and add in some cilantro.
8. Enjoy.

PUDIM DE LEITE CONDENSADO
Creamy Flan

Prep Time: 20 mins
Total Time: 3 hrs 15 mins

Servings per Recipe: 8
Calories	303 kcal
Fat	7.3 g
Carbohydrates	53.1g
Protein	7.9 g
Cholesterol	112 mg
Sodium	108 mg

Ingredients

- 1 C. white sugar
- 4 eggs, separated
- 1 (14 oz.) can sweetened condensed milk
- 3/4 C. milk, plus
- 2 tbsp milk

Directions

1. Set your oven to 350 degrees F before doing anything else.
2. In a heavy pan, add the sugar on low heat and melt for about 10 minutes, stirring continuously.
3. Immediately, place the sugar syrup into a round baking dish.
4. Tilt the dish to coat with the sugar syrup evenly and keep aside to cool.
5. In a blender, add the egg yolks and pulse on medium for about 5 minutes.
6. Add the condensed milk, 3/4 C. plus 2 tbsp of the milk and egg whites and pulse till all the ingredients are combined.
7. Place the egg mixture into the baking dish and with a foil paper, cover it.
8. Line a roasting pan with a damp kitchen towel and arrange the baking dish over the towel.
9. Place the roasting pan over the oven rack.
10. Add the boiling water in the roasting pan to reach halfway up the sides of the baking dish.
11. Cook in the oven for about 45-50 minutes or till a knife inserted 1-inch from the edge comes out clean.
12. Remove from the heat and keep aside to cool before unmolding onto a plate.
13. Refrigerate before serving.

Habichuelas Guisadas
Saucy Latin Beans

Prep Time: 20 mins
Total Time: 20 mins

Servings per Recipe: 4
Calories	170 kcal
Fat	5.2 g
Carbohydrates	23.8g
Protein	8.3 g
Cholesterol	2 mg
Sodium	580 mg

Ingredients
- 1 tbsp olive oil
- ¼ C. tomato sauce
- 2 tbsps sofrito
- 1 packet sazon seasoning
- ¼ tsp black pepper
- 2 C. cooked pinto beans, drained
- 1 ½ C. water
- salt to taste

Directions
1. For 5 mins heat and stir the following: pepper, oil, sazon, tomato sauce, and sofrito.
2. Combine in the salt, beans, and water.
3. Now turn up the heat to a medium level and cook everything for 20 mins.
4. Enjoy.

ARROZ CON POLLO
Chicken and Rice

🥣 Prep Time: 20 mins
⏰ Total Time: 2 hrs 5 mins

Servings per Recipe: 6
Calories   745 kcal
Fat   40.6 g
Carbohydrates   65.2g
Protein   30 g
Cholesterol   105 mg
Sodium   1926 mg

Ingredients

- 8 boneless chicken thighs, with skin
- ½ C. olive oil
- 2 C. diced onion
- 1 clove garlic, crushed
- ½ tsp crushed red pepper flakes
- 2 C. converted long-grain white rice
- 2½ tsps salt
- ½ tsp black pepper
- ¼ tsp saffron threads
- 1 can diced tomatoes
- 1 (4 oz.) can diced green chilis
- 1¼ C. chicken broth
- ¾ C. fresh peas
- 1 (4 oz.) jar pimentos, drained
- ½ (8 oz.) jar pimiento-stuffed green olives, drained and sliced
- ½ C. water

Directions

1. Set your oven to 325 degrees before doing anything else.
2. Begin to sear your chicken in olive oil then place the pieces to the side.
3. Now add to the same pot: your pepper flakes, onions, and garlic.
4. Let the mix cook for 7 mins then add the rice, saffron, pepper, and salt.
5. Toast the rice for 12 mins while stirring then add the broth, green chilies, and tomatoes.
6. Add the chicken thighs on top of everything and get the mix boiling.
7. Once everything is boiling, place a lid on the pot, and place the pot in the oven for 60 mins.
8. Now add the olives, pimentos, water, and peas.
9. Place the lid back on the pot and do not stir the contents.
10. Continue cooking everything for 25 mins.
11. Enjoy.

Tres Leches
Spanish 3 Milk Cake

Prep Time: 10 mins
Total Time: 1 hr

Servings per Recipe: 24
Calories	280 kcal
Fat	13.7 g
Carbohydrates	34.6 g
Protein	5.5 g
Cholesterol	81 mg
Sodium	87 mg

Ingredients

- 1 ½ C. all-purpose flour
- 1 tsp baking powder
- ½ C. unsalted butter
- 1 C. white sugar
- 5 eggs
- ½ tsp vanilla extract
- 2 C. whole milk
- 1 can sweetened condensed milk
- 1 can evaporated milk
- 1 ½ C. heavy whipping cream
- 1 C. white sugar
- 1 tsp vanilla extract

Directions

1. Coat a casserole dish with oil and flour then set your oven to 350 degrees before doing anything else.
2. Get a bowl, sift: baking powder and flour.
3. Get a 2nd bowl, combine: 1 C. sugar and butter. Then add: ½ tsp vanilla extract and eggs.
4. Combine both bowls and stir the mix until everything is smooth.
5. Enter the mix into your casserole dish and cook everything in the oven for 35 mins.
6. Now poke holes through the cake with a fork.
7. Get a 3rd bowl, combine: evaporated milk, condensed milk, and whole milk.
8. Pour the milk mix over the cake once it has cooled.
9. Get a 4th bowl, mix: 1 tsp vanilla, whipping cream, and 1 C. of sugar.
10. Coat your cake with the whipped cream mix then serve.
11. Enjoy.

SOFRITO
Spanish Spice Mix

Prep Time: 20 mins
Total Time: 20 mins

Servings per Recipe: 80
Calories   10 kcal
Fat   0.1 g
Carbohydrates   2.2g
Protein   0.4 g
Cholesterol   0 mg
Sodium   89 mg

Ingredients

2 green bell peppers, seeded and diced
1 red bell peppers, seeded and diced
10 ajies dulces peppers, tops removed
3 medium tomatoes, diced
4 onions, cut into large chunks
3 medium heads garlic, peeled
25 cilantro leaves with stems
25 leaves recao, or culantro
1 tbsp salt
1 tbsp black pepper

Directions

1. Blend the following with a blender: garlic, green peppers, onions, red peppers, tomatoes, red peppers, and ajies dulces.
2. Add in some black pepper, cilantro, salt, and the recao.
3. Continue blending until the mix resembles a salsa then place the contents in a sealable plastic container in the freezer.
4. Enjoy.

NOTE: To use the sofrito. Wait until the mix is frozen. Once it is frozen take the bag out of the freezer and scrape the ice with a tablespoon. Fill the tablespoon with the icy mix then add the scrapings into your dish as it cooks.

Tostones
Fried Spanish Plantains

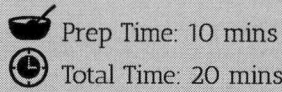

Prep Time: 10 mins
Total Time: 20 mins

Servings per Recipe: 2
Calories	136 kcal
Fat	3.3 g
Carbohydrates	28.5g
Protein	1.2 g
Cholesterol	0 mg
Sodium	14 mg

Ingredients

- 5 tbsps oil for frying
- 1 green plantain, peeled, diced into 1 inch pieces
- 3 C. cold water
- salt to taste

Directions

1. Get your oil hot and begin to fry your plantains for 4 mins each side.
2. Place the plantains on a working surface and flatten them.
3. After all of your plantains have been flattened dip them in some water then fry the plantains again for 1 min per side.
4. Top them with salt after frying.
5. Enjoy.

BISTEC ENCEBOLLAO
Steak and Onions

Prep Time: 15 mins
Total Time: 4 hrs 55 mins

Servings per Recipe: 6
Calories   423 kcal
Fat   32.1 g
Carbohydrates   6.3g
Protein   26.4 g
Cholesterol   81 mg
Sodium   587 mg

Ingredients

2 lbs beef sirloin steak, sliced thinly across the grain
½ C. olive oil
2 tbsps minced garlic
1 pinch dried oregano
1 (.18 oz.) packet sazon seasoning
2 large white onions, sliced into rings
¼ C. distilled white vinegar
1 C. beef stock
1 tsp salt

Directions

1. Get a bowl, combine: salt, steak, beef stock, olive oil, vinegar, garlic, onions, sazon, and oregano.
2. Place a covering of plastic over the dish after stirring the beef and place everything in the fridge for 5 hrs.
3. Add all of the mix into a large frying pan and get the mix boiling.
4. Once the mix is boiling, place a lid on the pan, set the heat to low, and cook everything for 45 mins.
5. Enjoy.

Bacalao Vizcaina
Codfish Soup

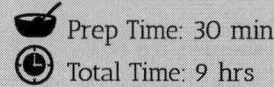 Prep Time: 30 mins
Total Time: 9 hrs

Servings per Recipe: 8
Calories	475 kcal
Fat	18.9 g
Carbohydrates	31.6 g
Protein	42.3 g
Cholesterol	192 mg
Sodium	4353 mg

Ingredients

- 1 lb salted cod fish, submerged in 2 qts of water, for 8 hours, change the water 4 times, then cut into small pieces
- 4 potatoes, sliced thick
- 2 onions, sliced
- 4 hard-boiled eggs, sliced
- 2 tsps capers
- 2 large cloves garlic, minced
- ¼ C. pitted green olives
- 1 jar roasted red bell peppers, drained
- ½ C. golden raisins
- 1 bay leaf
- 1 can tomato sauce
- ½ C. extra virgin olive oil
- 1 C. water
- ¼ C. white wine

Directions

1. Get a big pot and add in half of the following in layers: raisins, potatoes, roasted red peppers, fish, olives, onions, garlic, boiled eggs, and capers.
2. Now add in half of the tomato sauce and half of the olive oil.
3. Add the bay leaf and repeat the process.
4. Now add in the wine and the water.
5. Get everything boiling without stirring the mix.
6. Once everything is boiling place a lid on the pot and set the heat to low.
7. Let the contents cook for 35 mins.
8. Enjoy.

CLASSICAL
Spanish Beef Patties

Prep Time: 15 mins
Total Time: 45 mins

Servings per Recipe: 8
Calories	522 kcal
Fat	34.7 g
Carbohydrates	36.7g
Protein	15.9 g
Cholesterol	40 mg
Sodium	505 mg

Ingredients

3 tbsps olive oil
1 lb ground beef
1 ½ C. diced fresh cilantro
1 onion, diced
4 cloves garlic, minced
1 green bell pepper, diced
1 can tomato sauce
1 package egg roll wrappers
2 quarts vegetable oil for frying

Directions

1. Stir fry your bell pepper, onions, and garlic in olive oil until tender.
2. Combine in the meat and cook the meat until it is fully done.
3. Now add the cilantro and tomato sauce.
4. Heat the contents until the cilantro is soft then place everything to the side.
5. Now add 3 tbsps of the meat mix into an egg roll wrapper and shape the wrapper into a triangle.
6. Continue doing this until all your meat has been used up.
7. Now deep fry these patties in hot veggie oil until golden on both sides. Then place the patties on some paper towels before serving.
8. Enjoy.

Pupusas
Cheese Quesadillas from Salvador

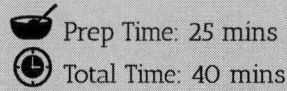
Prep Time: 25 mins
Total Time: 40 mins

Servings per Recipe: 4
Calories	297 kcal
Fat	7.3 g
Cholesterol	46.8g
Sodium	12.7 g
Carbohydrates	20 mg
Protein	85 mg

Ingredients
- 2 C. masa harina
- 1 C. water
- 1 C. queso fresco, crumbled

Directions
1. In a bowl, add the masa harina and water and mix till smooth.
2. With your hands, knead well.
3. Cover the bowl and keep aside for about 5-10 minutes.
4. Make 2-inch balls from the dough.
5. Place the dough onto a lightly floured surface and roll each ball into 6-inch round.
6. Place about 1/4 C. of the queso fresco over each round and cover with a second tortilla.
7. Pinch the edges together to seal the cheese.
8. Heat an ungreased nonstick skillet on medium-high heat and cook the tortillas, one at a time for about 2 minutes per side.

Karen's Reye's Spicy Chicken

 Prep Time: 20 mins
Total Time: 2 hrs 20 mins

Servings per Recipe: 8
Calories   483 kcal
Fat   31.6 g
Cholesterol   7.2g
Sodium   41.7 g
Carbohydrates 167 mg
Protein   385 mg

Ingredients

- 1 (5 lb.) whole chicken
- 2 C chicken broth
- 2 C water
- 1 C. Mexican crema
- 2 plum tomatoes, cut into 1/4-inch slices
- 2 red peppers, cut into 1-inch chunks
- 2 jalapeno peppers, sliced into rings
- 1 onion, cut into 1-inch chunks
- 2 cloves garlic, crushed
- 1 tsp dried oregano
- 1 bay leaf
- 1 pinch cayenne pepper
- salt and ground black pepper to taste
- fresh cilantro, chopped

Directions

1. In the bottom of a large pan, place the chicken, breast-side up.
2. Add the chicken broth, water, Mexican crema, tomatoes, red peppers, jalapeño peppers, onion, garlic, oregano, bay leaf, cayenne pepper, salt and pepper on medium heat and bring to a boil.
3. Reduce the heat to low and simmer, covered for about 1 hour.
4. With a pair of tongs, turn the chicken and simmer, covered for about 30 minutes.
5. Transfer the chicken into a plate and keep aside.
6. Increase heat to high and bring to a boil.
7. Cook for about 5-10 minutes, skimming off the fat from the top.
8. Cut the chicken into serving-size pieces and return to the pan.
9. Stir in the chopped cilantro and cook for about 5 minutes.

Costa Rican 5-Ingredient Potato Salad

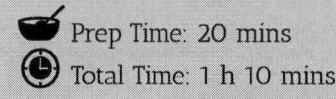

Prep Time: 20 mins
Total Time: 1 h 10 mins

Servings per Recipe: 6
Calories	212 kcal
Fat	7.2 g
Cholesterol	30.3g
Sodium	7.7 g
Carbohydrates	126 mg
Protein	219 mg

Ingredients
- 4 potatoes, peeled and cubed
- 1 (15 oz.) can sliced beets, drained and finely chopped
- 4 eggs
- 2 tbsp mayonnaise
- salt and pepper to taste

Directions
1. In a pan of the salted water, add the potatoes on high heat and bring to a boil.
2. Reduce the heat to medium-low and simmer, covered for about 20 minutes.
3. Drain well and let the potatoes steam dry for about 1-2 minutes.
4. Keep aside to cool completely.
5. Meanwhile in a pan, add the eggs in a single layer and enough water to cover on high heat.
6. Cover the pan and bring to a boil.
7. Remove from the heat and keep aside, covered for about 15 minutes.
8. Drain the eggs and rinse under running cold water to cool.
9. After cooling, peel and chop the eggs.
10. In a bowl, add the potatoes, beets, eggs, mayonnaise, salt and pepper and mix well.

JIBARITO
Sandwich in Fried Plantains Buns

Prep Time: 10 mins
Total Time: 25 mins

Servings per Recipe: 20
Calories   1219 kcal
Fat   100.4 g
Carbohydrates   165.4g
Protein   23.6 g
Cholesterol   68 mg
Sodium   551 mg

Ingredients

2 C. vegetable oil for frying
1 green plantain, peeled and halved lengthwise
2 tbsps vegetable oil
1 clove garlic, minced
4 oz. beef skirt steak, cut into thin strips
¼ medium yellow onion, thinly sliced
1 pinch cumin
1 pinch dried oregano

1 tbsp mayonnaise
1 slice processed American cheese, cut in half
2 slices tomato
3 leaves lettuce

Directions

1. Get 2 C. of veggie oil to 350 degrees then fry your plantains for 2 mins per side.
2. Place them on some paper towel then flatten them.
3. Now fry the flat plantains for 2 more mins then place them on the paper towels again.
4. Begin to stir fry your oregano, garlic, cumin, onion, and steak in 2 tbsps of oil until the steak is fully done.
5. Place a layering of mayo on one side of a plantain and then add some cheese, steak mix, tomato and lettuce.
6. Add another piece of plantain and cut the sandwich into two pieces.
7. Enjoy.

Full Latin Dinner
Chicken and Rice

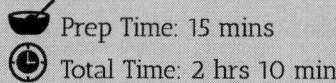

Prep Time: 15 mins
Total Time: 2 hrs 10 mins

Servings per Recipe: 8
Calories	535 kcal
Fat	20.2 g
Cholesterol	36.3g
Sodium	50.5 g
Carbohydrates	142 mg
Protein	1105 mg

Ingredients

- 1/4 C. vegetable oil
- 1 (4 to 6 lb.) whole chicken, cut into pieces
- 1 onion, chopped
- 1 green bell pepper, chopped
- 2 cloves garlic, minced
- 2 cloves garlic
- 1 (14.5 oz.) can stewed tomatoes
- 1 C. rice
- 2 tsp salt
- 1 tsp dried oregano
- 1/2 tsp ground black pepper
- 1 bay leaf
- 2 C. chicken stock
- 1 C. green peas
- 1/2 C. sliced black olives
- 1/2 C. raisins
- 1/4 C. chopped pimento peppers

Directions

1. Set your oven to 350 degrees F before doing anything else.
2. In a Dutch oven, heat the vegetable oil on medium heat and sear the chicken pieces for about 5-10 minutes.
3. With a slotted spoon, transfer the chicken pieces onto a plate.
4. In the same pan, add the onion, green bell pepper, minced garlic and whole garlic cloves and sauté for about 5 minutes.
5. Add the cooked chicken pieces, tomatoes, rice, salt, oregano, black pepper, bay leaf and enough chicken stock to cover the mixture.
6. Transfer the pan into the oven and cook for about 1 1/2 hours.
7. Stir in the peas, olives, raisins and pimento peppers and cook in the oven for about 15 minutes.

SAN SALVADOR
Butterflied White Fish

Prep Time: 20 mins
Total Time: 1 hr

Servings per Recipe: 6
Calories 534 kcal
Fat 27.2 g
Cholesterol 13.3g
Sodium 59.7 g
Carbohydrates 182 mg
Protein 159 mg

Ingredients

1/4 C. olive oil, divided
2 large whole white fish, butterflied, rinsed, and patted dry
1 tbsp garlic powder
salt and ground black pepper to taste
8 cloves garlic, minced
1/2 C. fresh lime juice
2 lemons, thinly sliced
2 Roma tomatoes, thinly sliced
1 Spanish onion, thinly sliced
1 green bell pepper, chopped

Directions

1. Set your oven to 4000 degrees F before doing anything else and grease a baking dish with 1 tsp of the olive oil.
2. Coat the fish fillets with the remaining olive oil evenly.
3. Arrange the fillets in the prepared baking dish and sprinkle with the garlic powder, salt and black pepper.
4. Spread the minced garlic over the fillets and drizzle with the lime juice.
5. Top with the lemon slices, tomato slices, onion slices and bell pepper slices.
6. With a piece of the foil, cover the baking dish tightly.
7. Cook in the oven for about 30-40 minutes.

Arroz Con Pollo
Chicken and Rice II

Prep Time: 25 mins
Total Time: 1 hr 35 mins

Servings per Recipe: 6
Calories   739 kcal
Fat   29.7 g
Carbohydrates   65.2 g
Protein   45.7 g
Cholesterol   136 mg
Sodium   198 mg

Ingredients

- ¼ C. vegetable oil, divided
- 6 chicken thighs, skinned and patted dry
- 6 chicken drumsticks with skin, patted dry
- salt and black pepper to taste
- 1½ bunches fresh cilantro, leaves picked from stems
- 6 cloves garlic, peeled and coarsely diced
- 1 aji (Peruvian) pepper, seeded and deveined
- 1 tbsp Worcestershire sauce
- ½ C. orange juice
- 2 C. uncooked white rice
- 2 onions, diced
- ½ C. white wine
- 3½ C. chicken broth
- 1 tsp freshly ground black pepper
- 1 large carrot, peeled and diced
- 1 bell pepper, any color, sliced into rings
- ¾ C. frozen peas

Directions

1. Begin to heat up two frying pans, each with 2 tbsps of veggie oil in them.
2. Coat your chicken with pepper and salt and divide the chicken between the pans.
3. Fry your chicken pieces for 17 mins then place them on some paper towels.
4. Now begin to process the following in a blender, until smooth: orange juice, cilantro leaves, Worcestershire, garlic, aji pepper, and garlic.
5. Add this mix to one of the pots and get it boiling.
6. Let the mix cook for 7 mins until it becomes a dark green color.
7. Now add your onions to the other pan and stir fry them for 7 mins then add in the rice

PLATANOS MADUROS
Fried Bananas II

Prep Time: 5 mins
Total Time: 15 mins

Servings per Recipe: 4
Calories   323 kcal
Fat   14.1 g
Cholesterol   51g
Sodium   1.8 g
Carbohydrates   0 mg
Protein   6 mg

Ingredients
2 large very ripe (black) plantains - peeled
1/4 C. vegetable oil
1 tbsp vanilla extract
1 tsp ground cinnamon
2 tbsp white sugar, or to taste (optional)

Directions
1. Cut each plantain into 2 halves and then each half into 3 strips.
2. In a large skillet, heat the vegetable oil on medium-high heat.
3. Gently, place the plantain strips in the skillet evenly.
4. Drizzle with the vanilla extract and sprinkle with the cinnamon.
5. Cook, covered for about 5-7 minutes per side.
6. Transfer the plantains onto a paper towel lined plate to drain.
7. Serve with a sprinkling of the sugar.

Carne Con Papas
Beef With Potatoes

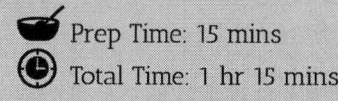

Prep Time: 15 mins
Total Time: 1 hr 15 mins

Servings per Recipe: 6	
Calories	611 kcal
Fat	35.3 g
Carbohydrates	20.4g
Protein	44.5 g
Cholesterol	132 mg
Sodium	1463 mg

Ingredients

- ½ green bell pepper, seeded and diced
- ½ small white onion, diced
- 3 cloves garlic, crushed
- ¼ tsp ground cumin
- ¼ tsp salt, divided
- 1/8 C. olive oil
- 1 tbsp olive oil
- 2 tbsps achiote powder
- 1 tsp ground cumin
- 2 (8 oz.) cans tomato sauce
- 2 lbs beef stew meat, cut into 1 inch cubes
- 2 white potatoes
- 1 C. white wine
- 4 C. water
- 6 cubes beef bouillon

Directions

1. Pulse the following with a blender: salt, green pepper, 1/4 tsp cumin, garlic, and onions.
2. Add in 1/8 C. of olive oil then continue processing the mix and place it to the side once everything is smooth.
3. Now add 1 tbsp of olive oil to a pressure cooker and heat it with a medium level of heat.
4. Begin to stir fry your green pepper mix for 2 mins then add in the achiote powder and 1 tsp of cumin.
5. Continue stir frying for 2 mins then add the tomato sauce.
6. Get everything gently boiling then combine in the beef and cook the meat for 7 mins before adding the water, bouillon, wine, and potatoes.
7. Get this mix boiling for 2 mins then place the lid on the cooker.
8. Cook the contents for 40 mins with 15 lbs of pressure.
9. Purge the steam from the pressure cooker and serve.
10. Enjoy.

HONDURAN BALEADAS
Avocado and Fried Bean Tacos

Prep Time: 25 mins
Total Time: 1 hr

Servings per Recipe: 8
Calories   390 kcal
Fat   23.1 g
Cholesterol   36.9 g
Sodium   10.1 g
Carbohydrates   43 mg
Protein   368 mg

Ingredients
Tacos:
2 C. all-purpose flour
1 C. water
1/2 C. vegetable oil
1 egg
1/2 tsp salt

Filling:
2 C. refried beans, warmed
1 avocado, sliced
1/2 C. crumbled queso fresco
1/4 C. crema fresca

Directions
1. In a large bowl, add the flour, water, vegetable oil, egg and salt and mix till a smooth dough is formed.
2. Make 8 golf ball-sized balls from the dough.
3. Cover the balls and keep aside for about 20 minutes.
4. Stretch each dough ball into a thick tortilla.
5. Heat a large skillet on medium-high heat and cook each tortilla for about 1 minute per side.
6. Place the refried beans, avocado and queso fresco over each tortilla evenly and drizzle with the crema.
7. Fold each tortilla in half over the filling.

Honduran Chicken Tacos w/ Tomato Sauce

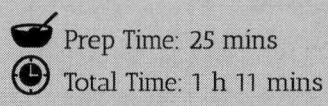

Prep Time: 25 mins
Total Time: 1 h 11 mins

Servings per Recipe: 5	
Calories	347 kcal
Fat	11 g
Cholesterol	49.4g
Sodium	15.6 g
Carbohydrates	23 mg
Protein	694 mg

Ingredients
- 2 skinless, boneless chicken breasts
- 1/2 tsp salt
- 1 tbsp vegetable oil
- 1 onion, finely chopped
- 1 tomato, finely chopped
- 1 green bell pepper, finely chopped
- 1 tsp chicken bouillon granules
- 1/2 tsp ground black pepper
- 1 lb corn tortillas
- vegetable oil for frying

Tomato Sauce:
- 1/4 C. water
- 1 (6.5 oz.) can tomato sauce
- 1/2 tsp chicken bouillon granules
- 1/2 tsp seasoned salt

Directions
1. In a pan, add the chicken breasts, salt in a pot and enough water to cover halfway and bring to a boil.
2. Cook for about 15 minutes.
3. Remove from the heat and keep aside to cool for about 5 minutes.
4. Shred the chicken breasts into thin pieces.
5. In a large skillet, heat 1 tbsp of the vegetable oil on medium heat and cook the onion, tomato and green bell peppers for about 2 minutes.
6. Stir in the shredded chicken, 1 tsp of the chicken bouillon and black pepper and cook for about 5 minutes.
7. Place some of the chicken mixture in the middle of each corn tortilla.
8. Fold each tortilla around the filling and secure with a toothpick.
9. In a large pan, heat the oil to 350 degrees F and fry the tortillas in batches for about 2 minutes per side.
10. Transfer the tortillas onto a paper towel lined plate to drain.
11. In a small pan, add 1/4 C. of the water and bring to a boil.
12. Add the tomato sauce, 1/2 tsp of the chicken bouillon and seasoned salt on medium-high heat and cook for about 5 minutes.
13. Place the sauce over the tacos and serve.

BEBIDA DE AVENA
South American Sweet Oat Drink

Prep Time: 10 mins
Total Time: 1 hr 15 mins

Servings per Recipe: 5
Calories 329 kcal
Fat 7.9 g
Cholesterol 54.4g
Sodium 8.3 g
Carbohydrates 27 mg
Protein 112 mg

Ingredients
6 C. water
1 C. rolled oats
2 C. cold water
1 (14 oz.) can sweetened condensed milk
2 tbsp vanilla extract
1 pinch ground cinnamon

Directions
1. In a tall pan, add the water and bring to a boil.
2. Add the oats and cook for about 5 minutes, stirring occasionally.
3. Remove from the heat and stir in the cold water, condensed milk and vanilla extract.
4. Transfer the oat mixture into a pitcher and refrigerate to chill for at least 1 hour.
5. Transfer the drink into the serving glasses and serve with a sprinkling of the cinnamon.

COSTA RICAN DINNER
Easy Picadillo
(Ground Beef and Plantains)

Prep Time: 20 mins
Total Time: 1 hr 10 mins

Servings per Recipe: 8
Calories	203 kcal
Fat	7.9 g
Cholesterol	29.8g
Sodium	6.1 g
Carbohydrates	24 mg
Protein	623 mg

Ingredients
4 plantains, peeled and cut into 3 pieces
1/2 lb. ground beef
2 cloves garlic, minced
2 tbsp minced onion
2 tsp salt
1/2 tsp pepper
1 1/2 tbsp chopped cilantro
1/2 C. tomato, chopped
2 tsp Worcestershire sauce
1 dash hot pepper sauce

Directions
1. In a pan of salted water, add the plantains on medium-high heat and cook till tender.
2. Drain well and keep aside to cool.
3. After cooling, chop the plantains finely.
4. In a large skillet, heat the oil on medium-high heat and cook the beef, garlic, and onion, salt and pepper till the beef is browned.
5. Stir in the chopped plantain, cilantro, tomato, Worcestershire sauce and hot pepper sauce and cook for about 10 minutes.

ISABELLA'S
Secret Belize BBQ Sauce

🥣 Prep Time: 20 mins
🕐 Total Time: 55 mins

Servings per Recipe: 16
Calories	42 kcal
Fat	0.1 g
Cholesterol	< 10.8g
Sodium	0.6 g
Carbohydrates	0 mg
Protein	137 mg

Ingredients
- 1 (16 oz.) can tomato sauce
- 1 large onion, chopped
- 2 habanero peppers, chopped
- 8 cloves garlic, minced
- 1 bunch cilantro, chopped
- 1 (16 oz.) can tomato paste
- 1 C. ketchup
- 1 C. honey
- 1 C. brown sugar
- 1/4 C. white vinegar

Directions
1. In a blender, add the tomato sauce, onion, habanero peppers, garlic and cilantro and pulse till smooth.
2. Add the tomato paste, ketchup, honey, brown sugar and white vinegar and pulse till smooth.
3. Transfer the sauce into a span on medium heat and cook for about 30-35 minutes, stirring occasionally.